Communication

A Poetic Approach

Communication
A Poetic Approach

Debilal Mishra

With a Foreword by
Prof. Srinivas Melkote

BLACK EAGLE BOOKS
Dublin, USA | Bhubaneswar, India

 Black Eagle Books
USA address:
7464 Wisdom Lane
Dublin, OH 43016

E-mail: info@blackeaglebooks.org
Website: www.blackeaglebooks.org

First International Edition Published by
Black Eagle Books, 2024

COMMUNICATION
by **Debilal Mishra**

Copyright © Debilal Mishra

All rights reserved. No part of this publication may be reproduced, stored in a retrieval system, or transmitted, in any form or by any means, electronic, mechanical, photocopying, recording or otherwise without the prior permission of the publisher.

Cover & Interior Design: Ezy's Publication

ISBN- 978-1-64560-509-6 (Paperback)
Library of Congress Control Number: 2024931204

Printed in the United States of America

Dedicated to

My Parents, Teachers and Students

Foreword

It gives me great pleasure and joy to write this foreword for *'Communication, a Poetic Approach,'* the forthcoming book of poems by Dr. Debilal Mishra.

It is with a joyful heart that I put pen to paper, or rather, fingers to keyboard, to try and capture the sheer force of his poetry. Words feel inadequate, but I must express the profound impact his verse has had on me.

There is originality in his work. He does not shy away from the gritty underbelly of existence, nor does he paint sanitized sunsets. His poems delve into the human labyrinth, exploring with equal grace the soaring peaks of humaneness and the cavernous depths of despair. His unflinching honesty, refusal to sugarcoat, is what compels me to enjoy each line, each image he summons in his poems.

Speaking of images, Dr. Debilal's poetry weaves different worlds so vividly that they leave my own senses reeling. I can literally smell the smoke of progress in his poems on communication, culture and development and feel the sting of injustice in his verses on forgotten faces and communities. His poems on development communication and artificial intelligence paint landscapes of the soul, landscapes both breathtaking and desolate.

His brilliance doesn't lie solely in sensory feasts. He

layers his poems with meaning, like Russian nesting dolls of the soul. Each reading peels back another layer, reveals another facet of a theme so multifaceted it takes one's breath away. Debilal challenges his readers, forcing them to think, to feel, to grapple with the complexities of what it means to be human.

In a world of fleeting tweets and soundbites, his poems are testaments to the power of language to move, to heal, to ignite. He is a sculptor of emotions, a cartographer of the unseen, and I am lucky to have stumbled upon his poetry.

On behalf of all the readers of his poetry, I thank Dr. Debilal for the gift of his art. Please keep weaving your tapestry of words, for the world desperately needs the light you shine through them.

I wish Dr. Debilal Mishra my best wishes and continued success in his future work.

Srinivas Melkote
Emeritus Professor
School of Media and Communication
Bowling Green State University, USA

Contents

Communication	11
The Message	13
Noise	14
Silence	15
The Voice	16
Perception	17
Culture	18
Development	19
Development Communication	20
Public Relations	22
Forwarded Wishes	24
Deleted Messages	25
The Stop	26
Happiness	27
The Last Day	28
Understanding	29
Trust	31
Humanity	32
Freedom	33
Am I Free?	35
The Journey	36
The Fortune	39
Artificial Intelligence	39
Are We Living	41
Celebration	43
Moments	44
Heart	45
The Colours	46
Example	47
Search	48
The Thought	49
Mother Earth	51

Life of a Journalist	52
Nostalgia	54
Fact	55
Sorry	56
Door	57
Never Remember	58
Epiphany	60
Story	61
Let's think like a Child again!	62
The Quarantine	64
Say to Yourself	65
The Mother	66
The Divinity	67
Daughter's Smile	68
Life	69
Failure	71
When You Love Someone	73
Rule of God	75
The Mahatma	76
Learning	77
Victory	79
Letter	80
Optimism	81
Aim and Pain	83
Religion	84
Possibility	85
Emotions	86
Relationship	88
Smile	89
My Body	90

Communication

Everything around us communicates
Through myriad senses and symbols;
Life is inconceivable
Without communication,
Since we survive
As long as we can communicate;

We connect, relate and reciprocate
Through communication,
And also we learn and grow;
Communication is central
To our conditions
As it helps us exist
And sustain the relationships;
Communication is not a mere act
Of sending and receiving messages;
Rather, it's a behavior
As natural as nature;
A storm or stream,
Silence or rush,
It's capable of both
Creation and devastation,
It can kill
It can heal
Carrying such massive energies of the universe;
Communication connects at some point

Where the intent engenders trust
Beyond the content;
Communication leads to relationship
And both share reciprocal effects;
Or rather, the nature of the communication
Is determined by the nature of the relationship
And the nature of the relationship
Is determined by the nature of the communication;

To communicate is to understand
For both go together,
Communication, in essence, is a process
Of sharing something meaningfully,
And achieving mutual understanding,
Based on some contextual commonness;

It takes some commonness
Between the communicators
To achieve mutual understanding,
And some degrees of appreciation and acceptance
Can make the difference,
And add to the beauty
Of the unfading experience!

"Communication is a process of sharing something meaningfully and achieving mutual understanding based on some contextual commonness"

The Message

There are not just words in it
Rather, it's more of an experience
Of the consciousness,
The message is born
With the understanding
Of the inner essence;

The beauty of the message
Consists in the beauty of the mind
Free from all noise and barriers,
Since it is the life of all communications
And the base of all behaviours,
Encoded and decoded
Along the sensible symbols
Of the life's matters;
It can be as soothing as a flower
And as devastating as fire,
The message is never small;
It carries an intrinsic intent
And a colossal power!

••

"The beauty of the message consists in the beauty of the mind"

Noise

Noise disturbs the silence
Noise distorts the meaning
Noise dispels peace
There's noise in the medium
There's noise in the mind
There's noise in the behaviour
All noise interferes with understanding
And disrupts the communication
If there's noise,
There can be no effective encoding or decoding
Of the sense of the message,
The real noise comes with ignorance
And goes with knowledge!

●●

"The real noise comes with ignorance and goes with knowledge"

Silence

Silence has its own sound,
Quite prolific and profound
It's never 'no communication',
Rather, it's the veiled intention
That signifies the deeper essence;
It may be the truth,
It may be pretence;

Silence communicates
More than the words,
It's a language in itself
That carries myriad symbols
Of the indomitable emotion;
The silence vibrates the soul,
And resonates the psychic reflection!

"Silence is a language in itself"

The Voice

There's a voice in everything;
In every emotion,
Of every being;
Some voices are resonant,
And some are silent,
But every voice tries to express
The deeper essence of Life;
It takes an ear to hear,
A mind to listen;
And a soul to feel the voice;
The voice grows with time,
It transcends
The mundane boundaries
Of the communion;
And keeps vibrating through
The inner space of the human sensibility
In every season!

●●

"There is a voice in everything"

Perception

There can be no meaning without perception
And there can be no perception
Without contextual impression;
I perceive you
The way you impress me
The contextual impression consists in
Experience, learning, awareness and feeling;
Someone's perception
Makes things meaningful to them,
Perception is always individual
There can be no universal perception
Since everyone has got their own unique ways
ultimately;
Perception can drive the personality
And affect the performance;
But performance can change the perception
And occasion a deviance!

●●

"I perceive you the way you impress me"

Culture

Culture consists in everything
We experience
Within the confines
Of the consciousness;
Culture is what we are,
Or rather, all the ways
We think and behave;

Culture forms the core
Of the character
And acts as the primary
Pattern of existence;

Culture is learned, valued,
And communicated
Through the shared symbols
In a society,
As an integrated complex whole
Culture vibrates the social life
And the individual goal!

●●

"Culture forms the core of the character"

Development

Development is always a process
Of positive change
That is participatory and inclusive in nature
And is led by a collective conscience;

Development can never be an imposition;
Rather, it's a crucial transformation
Of the consciousness into character,
And of the character into culture;

The process begins with concern,
Grows through conviction,
Thrives on the values
Of commitment and consistency,
And becomes complete
With change,
Both within and without;

Development, as a never-ending process,
Calls for reciprocal action and access
In the larger interest;
It can never stop
Since every voice matters
And every step counts!

●●

"Development, as a never-ending process, calls for reciprocal action and access in the larger interest"

Development Communication

Communication for development
Essentially involves
Conscience, consciousness and character;

Development communication aims at
Creating a positive change
By way of a
Positive content and
A positive intent;

It's more of a process
Of listening to the inner voice
And communicating the experience
Meaningfully to cause
A desired behaviour;

In a sense,
Development communication
Is centred on love,
Either for the message,
Or for the audience, or both;

It certainly takes a lot of character
To communicate for Development,
For being sensitive, receptive and connective In
the environmental context
Is not everyone's cup of tea;

Development communication,

In its essence,
Is a ceaseless journey
Of relationship-building;

That's to say,
Communication creates relationships
And relationships facilitate development;

Change causes change
If change is the target,
Change is the asset;
Development communication
Is a way to harmonize,
The content and intent
In the greater human interest;
With some passion
And commitment!

●●

"Development communication aims at creating a positive change by way of a positive content and a positive intent"

Public Relations

Public Relations essentially involves
A process of Relationship-building
Based on communication, trust,
Understanding, acceptance and character;
We can't accept something
As long as we don't trust them
Trust leads to acceptance,
Acceptance leads to relationship,
And relationship alone can
Facilitate persuasion
That is the ultimate goal;
Positive intention, honest communication,
And the responsible behavior
Constitute the trust
Without which no relationship
Can ever exist;
The process of Public Relations
Begins with research,
Since research leads to understanding,

Of the public and the medium,
That makes the communication effective;
The process is never complete
Without evaluation of the public attitude!

●●

"Public Relations essentially involves a process of relationship-building based on communication, understanding, trust, acceptance and character; since we can't accept something as long as we don't trust them"

Forwarded Wishes

Forwarding a message
To wish someone
Carries little effort,
And unwinds the sender's intention
Devoid of any genuine emotion;

Every person is unique
And so is every relationship
If the relationships can't be forwarded,
How can the messages be?

Nothing is the same
In the 'same-to-you' and 'Same-here'
Since every emotion has its own labour;
If you forward a wish,
Given by someone,
To someone else,
You are never involved
In the process!

●●

"Nothing is the same in the 'same-to-you' and 'same-here'…"

Deleted Messages

The deleted messages
Sometimes sparkle some
Subtler senses,
They flabbergast my innocent face
And my mind is led
Into a deeper recess;

Is it your conscience that deletes it?
Or it is your lurking arrogance!
No feelings can ever be hidden
In a relationship made of love
If pretence is the source,
The words meet the fateful curve
Of the destiny your thoughts enforce;

Misunderstanding is never caused
By mere words and language,
Rather, it results more from the attitude
And its parochial bondage;
Before deleting the messages therefore,
Let's learn to explore ourselves
More and ever more!

●●

"Misunderstanding is never caused by mere words and language; rather, it results more from the attitude and its parochial bondage"

The Stop

Nothing stops
At a stop,
But the elusive illusion;

Every stop
Is a new start
In understanding life
And perceiving the world;

It›s an occasion to learn
And realize the inner strengths
And weaknesses;

Moreover, it›s another chance
To gather oneself
And move forward!

●●

"Every stop is a new start in understanding the life and perceiving the world"

Happiness

Happiness lies within
It can't be found without
You may invest everything
But in the end
Only you can make yourself happy;
You can't buy it
You can't sell it
It's something you can only feel and realize
Once you become
One with the deeper self,
Beyond any shape or size;

It's a choice,
And is always in the offing,
If you can connect to yourself
From within,
The signals of happiness
Will never go missing!

●●

"If you can connect to yourself from within, the signals of happiness will never go missing"

The Last Day

Nothing ends in the world
Since the memories last forever
Life is such a beautiful journey
Full of events and wonder;
Some moments may be tougher
And some may be sweet,
But the urge to love and live
Must continue
Through both darkness and light;
There's someone special
Inside everyone,
Nothing can ever stop
The torrent of a tremendous will
And all that it can;
The time goes on
There can be no last day
The Sun will rise again
With an even brighter ray!

●●

"There is always someone special inside everyone"

Understanding

Without understanding
Every experience is miserable,
Understanding makes life complete and meaningful;

Lack of understanding
Can cause colossal crises
It can play havoc with the relationships
And strip the life of its essence;
Misunderstandings mostly occur
To a closed mind,
Full of perceptions of its own kind,
And the greater degrees of ego
And self-conceit
Further add to the inner whirlwind;
When we can't understand

There's no problem,
We may again try;
But, when we don't want to understand
Nothing can help it,
The whole world may cry!
Every mind is unique
And so are its ways,
The lack of the ability to understand
Is not as perilous as
The lack of the needful interest and mindful effort;

Understanding lies in love
It is replete with sensitivity
And patience,
Understanding is never a piece of cake;
It's a deeply conscious process!

●●

"Understanding is not a piece of cake; it's a deeply conscious process"

Trust

Trust is a gargantuan power
It can bind the soul
It can find the goal
And it can cause
The most arduous overhaul;
Trusting nothing is despair
Trusting something is hope
The inner trust is strength;
That is trusting the
Incredible possibilities
And unbounded energies within;
If you can't trust yourself,
You are not yourself;
The real trust lies inside
It helps explore
The real self that sustains
Life's true essence!

●●

"If you can't trust yourself, you are not yourself"
"The inner trust is strength"

Humanity

Humanity has no identity,
It's not confined to any caste, race, religion, gender, creed, culture and group;
It lies in the essence of love and sensitivity;
In a heart filled with the unalloyed feelings
Of compassion;

Humanity is never slender
It's as vast as the universe,
Open and profound from within,
It takes a lot of character to be human;
Mere physical characteristics are not enough;
Since it sustains the human connectivity
As central to the human progress,

Humanity lies in the values of life
And at the core of the realization
Of the deeper self,
That sustains the conscience,
And urges to rise into the higher consciousness!

●●

"It takes a lot of character to be human"

Freedom

In freedom lies
The essence of life,
Beyond the shadow
Of all sordid strife,
Life thrives on freedom
And freedom grows with life;
Both making each other
Meaningfully ripe;

Freedom has no form
It's all nature,
A sense of purity
In the thoughts that matter;

Freedom consists in the
Inner positive being
That lets the heart dance
And urges the soul to sing,
With the ever-mystic vibrations of life;

You are the master of your own freedom
None can take it away
Neither can it cause any harm
Since it lives within
And exists as a conscientious force
Of the consciousness;

Freedom can be felt
By being aware of the self,
And the prodigal immortality
In the ever deeper depth!

●●

"Life thrives on Freedom, and Freedom grows with Life"

Am I Free?

When my sweat stops my soul
When I can't think beyond the goal
When my smile remains silent
And the circumstances tend to judge my element,
I ask myself: Am I Free?

When my mind grows a sight weaker
When my thoughts make me falter
When my conscience is full of fear
And all my strength bursts into tear,
I ask myself: Am I Free?

When I forget my inner divinity
When I am lured into the mundane frivolity
When I can't express my own substance
And seek after extrinsic dependence,
I ask myself: Am I Free?

When I get trounced by my emotion
When my self-belief can no longer function
When I can't withstand the inner commotion
And prefer to forgo the right action,
I ask myself: Am I Free?

●●

"Am I really free when I can't express my inner divinity?"

The Journey

Drinking a glass of the mystic sweat
Mixed with the love's blood
The soul aspires to move again
Along life's adverse road;

The journey seems interminable
The footsteps and footprints aren't matching anymore
The blue sky has turned black
Amidst the dog's gruesome bark;

The vivid memories stand on the way
Confronting the move of the mind
The friendly fear smiles
At the unending miles
The emotional pandemic still is not over
The destiny is yet to suffer
From some unseen fever
That is growing within
With the hope's reduced temperature;

The hands can feel the essence of pain
In holding the load of the precious emotions
The legs aren't the same anymore
They have become the pillars of expectations!!!

The journey is no more a journey
It's a revelation of the human truth
That remains in every dream
And keeps to the warmth
Of every breath;

Life is not always the favourite season
The seasons change,
And the life lives again!
Come hell or high water
No migration can ever occur within
As long as the love for life continues
And the hope prevails over poverty;

The Apocalypse has left the soul sweating all the way;
And the sweat speaks to the soul
Rethinking the goal,
It's not yet time for sleep
More to run,
And more to roll!

"Life is not always the favourite season: the seasons change, and the life lives again!"

The Fortune

I may weep for years,
My tear-drops can't bring my fortune;
I may not utter a word,
My silence can't bring my fortune;
All the quagmires in the mind,
And all the morbid sentimentality that I find;
While musing on my past
And indulging in my dream;
Can't ever bring my fortune;
My fate can't make me great,
the greatness of my effort matters;
My fervent love for the efforts,
And the dare and desire
To look beyond the excuses,
Lead my being to an unseen pleasure,
And there lies my fortune;
And its unceasing fervor!

●●

"My fate can't make me great, the greatness of my effort matters"

Artificial Intelligence

The human intellect
Is no longer limited to
The ordinary human experiences;
It has evolved
Into a more complex version of reality
That encompasses
The augmented patterns of the human lives,
Propelled by the technological dynamics
Of the intellect,
And the intellectual dynamics of the technology;

The reciprocal effects of
The man-machine relationship
Have altered the equations of
The human communication
Within the civilizational frontiers,
Giving rise to the disparate
Sets of identities
Leading to a new culture
Shaping the distinct social sensibilities;

Technology is beneficial
As long as it doesn't create
 A sense of extreme human dependency
Or doesn't take away the moral possessions of the human mind;

Since nothing can ever replace
The human vibrations in the world of the humans;
Intelligence can never be artificial
If the mind is still alive and thinks like a human
Technology is helpful as a medium
Not as a boss of the mind;

The nature of the use is always
Determined by the nature of the user,
And that the larger benefits
Of any medium rest inevitably
On the soundness of our minds!

●●

"The nature of the use is always determined by the nature of the user; and the larger benefits of any medium rest inevitably on the soundness of our minds"

Are We Living

Are we really living?
With a stressful face
And such a massive race,
Of loss and gain
Full of hurt and pain;
And without a moment's healing
Are we really living?
No time for a friend,
Life's knackered no end,
The words are tough
The mind is rough;
And without enjoying
Are we really living?

Exuding more negativity,
Blocking all creativity,
Competing with others,
Ignoring the inner powers;
And with all fear and misgiving
Are we really living?
The heart is drained,
Of beauty and compassion
The soul is empty,
Of purity and passion
The dreams are dry
And the emotions cry;

Without the humane feeling
Are we really living?

● ●

"Without a moment's healing, are we really living?"

Celebration

Let's celebrate
Life's every moment,
With no loss of vigour and joy,
Amidst its entire predicament!
Let's learn from the experiences
Bitter or sweeter,
Life is a story of choice and character;
A story of the journey
And when and where we stop
And start trying again;
Life is a matter of living
In all seasons,
We may or may not like all
But we must get hold of ourselves
Both in spring and fall;
Life gives us challenges
To explore what we truly are
And find the meaning of the existence
Amidst all commotion;
With love, smiles, hopes and dreams
And above all, the unflinching faith
In the astounding inner strength,
Life goes on
As an unfailing celebration!

●●

"Life is a story of choice and character: a story of the journey and when and where we stop and start"

Moments

The moments are born
Of the passion of the soul
The journey begins
With the love
For the Goal;

The depth of the dream
Causes the flurry,
The beauty of the efforts
Results in glory;
The path to glory
Is full of pain,
Now is the Sun,
Now is the rain
The life is only for the brave to live,
More to go and more to give!

"The life is only for the brave to live, more to go and more to give"

Heart

Your heart is precious
Love it,
Live it,
Listen to it,
And Keep it with you forever;

Never give it to anyone
They may not deserve it
Don't sell your heart
Since it carries priceless emotions,
Never put it on a deal
Always let it feel
Your flowering love
In the essence of its verve;
Care for it more and evermore
Don't let anyone break or steal it
For nothing is rarer than its core;

Your heart smiles with you
Your heart cries with you
It makes you yourself
And it comes and goes with you...

●●

"Your heart smiles with you; your heart cries with you; it makes you yourself; and it comes and goes with you"

The Colours

May the colours of love
Never fade from life,
Let there be peace and progress
And no sordid strife!

May the colours of the self-belief
Stay there forever,
Let the mightier hope prevail
Over all mundane fever;

May the colours of the dreams
Ever glorify the efforts,
Let there be no failure,
With constant perseverance
And focus;

May the colours of the unflinching faith
Create indelible miracles,
Let there be a plethora of
The positive vibes
To overcome all obstacles!

●●

"The colours of the unflinching faith create indelible miracles"

Example

The ocean is calm, wide and deep
No waves can ever stir its sleep
Let the heart have the depth of the ocean
No emotion can ever inflict pain;

The storm sounds horrible
Yet survives the bubble
Though it is to live for a flash
It has a presence before the lash;
A stormy presence
That never ceases
The urge and effort to create life
Amidst the ever brutal strife;

The Moon is lonely
Yet full of spark,
Alone in the sky
It dispels the dark,
Life has to shine like the Moon
May it be a bane or a boon!

●●

"Let the heart have the depth of the ocean, no emotion can ever inflict pain"

Search

When you miss something
Never feel derelict;
Rather, see into the depth of your heart,
And listen to the immortal stories
Devoid of wounds and worries,
Try to stand even stronger
Without fear or anger,
The road is never always straight
Still the journey can be great
If you can move with the best find
And leave the rest behind,
Let the dark do you strong,
If there's a soul
There's a song,
Nothing can ever devour the light,
The bigger is the faith
The smaller is the fight!

●●

"Let the dark do you strong; if there is a soul, there is a song"

The Thought

Never believe that
You are weak or poor,
Or you are defeated,
Or have lost the battle;
You are just a thought away!
Think that you have it in you
And you can be yourself always,
You are capable of loving the world
Even if it is full of hatred;
Your purity, passion and positivity
Can create new hopes
Amidst life›s colossal darkness;

Never believe that
The time is bad,
Or the fortune is far away!
You are just a thought away!
Believe that you are the maker
Of your own destiny,
And master of your moments;
Think that you can rise
Beyond all reasons,
And that you can continue
With your journey
In all seasons;

Never believe that
You can't dream,
Or you can't reach the goal,
Or you don't have what
It takes to be there;
You are just a thought away!
Think that you are made for
Greater heights,
Which you can scale
Only through the bigger fights!

●●

"You are the maker of your own destiny and master of your own moments"

Mother Earth

She is not just a piece of land,
She is my Life's life,
The mother Earth,
She sustains my presence,
And causes my essence;

She bears everything
I love and hate,
And everything that makes me
Crawl, stand, dream, rise and fall,
She is the mother Earth,
The spring of my breath and soul;

She leads me to feel,
Sense and imagine
My existence and beyond,
With a lot of character;
She is the mother Earth,
The wellhead of my creations,
And my ultimate creator!

●●
"The mother Earth is my ultimate creator"

Life of a Journalist

I am a journalist,
My mother often scolds me,
For I never return home in time,
My father gets angry silently
Since I forget everything that's mine;

My wife rings me
To have lunch,
But, I never receive;
She cries unseen tears
And I prefer to deceive;

I can't keep my promises
Made to someone special,
I keep hurting their feelings,
But, they still love me
And I feel bad for their love
Which I hardly deserve;

I am perceived differently
By different people,
Some praise me
Some pity me
Some hate me
And some exploit me,
Yet I run after the pulses of time;

I am made of some stony stuff
Bereft of sensations,
I can't feel my pain,
Even I can't express my emotions,
Since I know my deadline
And go my agenda;

I am a journalist
Despite all my grumbles
I feel happy,
When my pen brings smiles
On some painful faces,
And here lies my real identity
Where all my anguish lapses!

"Despite all my grumbles, I feel happy when my pen brings smiles on some painful faces; and here lies my real identity where all my anguish lapses"

Nostalgia

Nothing has changed,
But something is missing;

The people are the same,
The places are the same,
The stories are the same,
And the same life is flowing,
But something is missing;

The same words are around,
The same images are found,
The same faces are smiling,
But something is missing;

Life takes myriad shapes
Dreams, parties and the cakes
Of the celebrations that go on,
For the perennial mundane fun;
And in the décor of the emotions
Nothing has changed,
But something is missing!

●●

"In the décor of the emotions nothing has changed, but something is missing"

Fact

You can block me,
You can shock me,
You can unfriend,
You can mute me,
But you can't delete me
From your heart,
And it's a fact;

You may not add me,
You may not follow me,
You may not confirm,
You may reject me,
But you can't delete me
From your heart,
And it's a fact;

I am a feeling
Growing within
As a rhythm
That keeps you thinking
And you too know it
While breathing,
But you can never share that,
And it's a fact!

●●

"You can never delete me from your heart, and it's a fact"

Sorry

When we don't say sorry
To someone
After making a mistake,
We don't need them;

When we say sorry
To someone
After making a mistake,
We need them;

When we say sorry
To someone
Even without making a mistake,
We love them;

Only love can lead us
To sacrifice our ego
And liberate ourselves!

●●

"Only love can lead us to sacrifice our ego and liberate ourselves"

Door

When the door is closed
Let's never stop trying,
A strong door is always there
For a greater fortune
And it takes an equally greater effort to open;

Tough times test the character
And offer opportunities
To discover the inner strengths;

The door to success
Opens through effort, commitment and conviction;
Moreover, rejections refine us,
Difficulties define us,
And dreams determine us!

•●

"Tough times test the character and offer opportunities to discover the inner strengths"

Never Remember

Never remember
The bad memories
That keep blocking your mind
And stop you from finding yourself;

Never remember
The experiences that make you
Fragile from within
And forbid you from blooming
Into your dreams;

Never remember
The wounding words of someone
You love and adore
For love is more precious than anything;

Never remember
Those emotions that take over
Your strengths
And let you doubt your worth;

Life is all about believing and living again
In every season
One may like or not,

The journey must be celebrated every moment
May it be long or short!

● ●

"Life is all about believing and living again in every season"

Epiphany

The moment we realize
That we are unique,
We grow bigger
Than our worries;

Life never affects
All alike,
The nature of perception
Makes a great difference;

Life can be beautiful
When we replace
Fear with faith,
Pain with patience,
Loathing with love,
Despair with dreams,
And ego with enlightenment!

●●

"The moment we realize that we are unique, we grow bigger than our worries"

Story

We all are unique,
And so are our stories,
Every story has the power
To connect and inspire;
A story is more of a character,
It's certainly different
The way we are;

Your story can change lives
If it is replete with
Purpose, passion and perseverance;

And a beautiful story
Largely results
From the beauty
Of the relationship with life!

"Every story has the power to connect and inspire"

Let's think like a Child again!

Let's think like a child again!
Let's laugh,
Let's cry,
Let's sing under the Sun
And dance in the rain;

All those memories of
The mystic moments,
Amidst the purity of the pulse,
And the aura of the artless breath,
Are always alive and frequent
 The deeper emotions' ocean,
Let›s think like a child again;

Those irreproachable thoughts,
That would urge to be ourselves,
Beyond the realm of the fruitless ego,
Often implore the heart to loosen
The grip of the unseen chain,
Let›s think like a child again;

Let›s love the moments,
Let›s live the moments,
And let›s be free within,
To create the moments;
And let's feel the pleasure of the

Innocent pain,
Let›s think like a child again!

● ●

"Let's feel the pleasure of the innocent pain, let's think like a child again"

The Quarantine

We may be quarantined
But our souls are not,
They still keep with each other
Being the strength and depth
Of some subtler ardour;

The abstruse virus can›t
Ever infect our love
And the miraculous myriad emotions;
This is certainly a testing time
For our silent faith
And adoring aspirations;

The moment has made us
Even stronger
And even nearer are we;
Nothing can ever create
An arduous vacuum
Between you and me!

●●

"We may be quarantined, but our souls are not"

Say to Yourself

Say to yourself:
'I am immensely capable
And beautiful the way I am,
Come hell or high water,
I am here for me forever';

Say to Yourself:
'Nothing can stop me ever
I am my eternal lover
No hate or hurt
Can ever make a difference
To my world full of wonder';

Say to Yourself:
'I can drink all pain,
I can erase every stain
From my destiny
That I can certainly gain
 On the strength of
My sweat and strain!'

●●

"Nothing can stop me ever, I am my eternal lover"

The Mother

You are the life of the life,
O Mother!
Carrying the warmth of love
That energizes the soul,
You live in the subtlety
Of the sensations of the heart,
And let the world rise in your prayers;

You are the mother,
The master communicator,
But you keep calm
In yourself;
In the depth of
The unsaid emotions;

You expect nothing,
Since you believe in giving,
Turning all the pain into paradise,
Both in the summer and spring!

●●

"You are the master communicator and you let the world rise in your prayers"

The Divinity

The desires often travel into
The darkness of the being
Causing a bitter tremor;
The light of thy knowledge
Is the only redeemer
From the bondage of
The mundane string;

Life seeks peace of the soul
That is found nowhere,
The thirst of devotion is unquenched
Before the ego's glare;
Thine love is the only solace
To expand into the spirit of the Truth;
And to move forward and ever forward
On the expedition into the inner recess,
Where lies the beauty
And joy of being selfless!

●●

"The Divine knowledge is the only redeemer from the bondage of the mundane string"

Daughter's Smile

She doesn't need anything,
She only needs a heart
Of pure love;
She thinks for you
She cries for you
But hides everything
Behind her smile;

At times she fights
Sometimes she complains,
But mostly she loves
And never forgets her duties;
She swallows all her pain,
But her smile
Makes you happy!

She understands everything,
When you are sad,
She never expresses her needs
She acts like your mother;
And her smile
Makes you cry within!

●●

"She acts like your mother; and her smile makes you cry within"

Life

Life is often heard in the
Subtle echo of the prayers,
And in the depth of the unseen tears;
Life is often seen in
The dreams of the countless people
Who spend sleepless nights,
Beneath the warmth of their hopes;

Life is often felt in the
Struggle to survive,
In the instinct to thrive,
And the passion to achieve
The goals made of the sweat
Of the myriad emotions;

Life is often lived
In the celebration of the moments
That indeed carry the life's essence;
Life smiles in the smile
Of an innocent heart
That beats with love;

Life never lies in the mundane indulgence
And its sordid surface size,
Life grows ever beautiful

With the beauty of the thoughts
And the purity of the efforts on the rise!

●●

"Life grows ever beautiful with the beauty of the thoughts and the purity of the efforts"

Failure

O Failure, kindly visit me
And show your hideous face,
I want to see it,
And win the life's race!

O Failure, visit me for pity's sake
And give your bitter taste,
I want to have it,
And raise me the best!

O Failure, visit me once
And unveil your essence,
I want to learn from you,
And touch all excellence!

O Failure, do visit me
And cast your demonic spell,
I want to live it,
And come out of my shell!

O Failure, visit me must
And come to your liking,

But I know you'll never,
Since I am still learning and trying!

●●

"O Failure, visit me must and come to your liking, but I know you'll never, since I am still learning and trying"

When You Love Someone

When you love someone
Don't say 'I love you',
Don't expect 'I love you too' either;
If there is love,
It takes care of everything;

Love is as natural as life
It's devoid of all strife
Don't try to possess love,
It can't be possessed
It's not an obsession
Don't be foolishly obsessed;

Never try to claim or demand it,
Or prove or certify it either;
It's a mystic feeling
Of the divine energy
That exists within;

Love never limits yourself,
Love leads you to know yourself
Love lets you grow,
Love lets you rise
It never lets you fall,
It never lowers your size
If you need it,

It isn't love
When you live it,
It is love;
Love is love only
It is made of love
If you force it into anything,
It is no longer love...

●●

"If there's love, it takes care of everything"

Rule of God

The preciosity of the humanity
Is the quintessence of all religions
And sacred texts,
Humanity is exploring the divinity within;

Life is beautiful
Beyond all sordid strife,
Actions spring from the thoughts
And thoughts must
Meet the love unalloyed,
And the deeper divine light,
Causing the true growth of the being
In the interest of the creation,
Where the rule of God
Shall continue,
Through everyone's inner perfection;

Nothing is needed for Him
For He loves to reside
In the hearts of those
Who are as pure as their Gods;
He loves to be human yet again,
Since humanity is the ultimate goal
And life's measuring rod!

●●

"Humanity is the ultimate goal and life's measuring rod"

The Mahatma

Creating the herculean harmony
Among the discordant thoughts
You set the path for the inner freedom;

Discovering the tremendous strength
Of Truth and Non-violence
You gave the humankind
A newer revelation;

You taught the art of
Celebrating values
Through exploring the self
By living within;
You could invoke
An extraordinary power
In the character
Of an apparently ordinary being!

••

"There is a tremendous strength in Non-violence"

Learning

I am still a small kid
In the Life's university,
I am trying to learn some lessons
From each and every opportunity;

Life has taught me
To love myself evermore
Since this love is unalloyed
And innocent to the core;

Life has taught me
Not to expect, or compete
Or compare,
For this will kill the real essence;
I must explore myself instead
And enjoy the journey;

Life has taught me
Not to give up on things
I want to achieve for a cause;
It has also taught me that
Failure is only a state of mind,
And that the mind must be
Having an ever positive urge;

Life has taught me
That there is a great joy
In making someone smile
Maybe in smaller ways,
And spreading the happiness;
And that the real life lies
In a beautiful heart
Beyond all complexes!

●●

"The real life lies in a beautiful heart"

Victory

They talk about the greatest victories
And those who are victorious;

Life gives chances,
To emerge victorious
Through the efforts to overcome
The weaknesses within;

Hardships test the patience
And the commitment to strive harder,
Life grows bigger
Beyond the imagination;

And the victory over the self
Is a matter of character
And ceaseless self-motivation!

"Life gives chances to emerge victorious through the efforts to overcome the weaknesses within"

Letter

Here is a letter to myself!

Hope you are full of love and light,
And in search of your own delight,
You must explore your deeper self
Since here lies your greater faith;

Hope you are not spreading hate
Or being unkind
You may not love or trust all though;
Hope you are not growing intolerant
And losing your mind;

The shape of the world may change,
But your soul must remain the same;
Never let the sordid glitter
Erode you from within,
Come fire or fame!

●●

"The shape of the world may change, but the soul must remain the same"

Optimism

All the agony of the struggle
Will melt in the depth
Of the desired destination,
The journey must continue
Through the sweat and sweetness
Of life ceaselessly,
The beloved dreams one day
Will overcome the lovers' pain,
Hold on, O Brave heart!
The world will be better again;

This time will be over sooner
Since nothing can last longer
Beyond its own time,
The sin and the sinner
Will see the salvation together
In the deeper recess
Of the nature's rhyme;
And the morning of the sun
Will prevail over the cloud of the rain,
Hold on, O Brave heart!
The world will be better again;

Know the power of the prayers
And the strength of the soul
Harder is the effort,

Closer is the goal,
A committed mind
Can break the biggest chain,
Hold on, O Brave heart!
The world will be better again…

●●

"This time will be over sooner since nothing can last longer beyond its own time"

Aim and Pain

If there's an aim,
There's a pain;
The higher is the aim,
The deeper is the pain;

Life wants us to
Live the pain
And love it,
For the pain greatly purges
The path to the aim,
That makes life meaningful;

Both pain and aim
Make each other
Ever more beautiful
And add Life to the life!

●●

"The higher is the aim, the deeper is the pain"

Religion

Beyond the toxic vicious mesh,
The heart of the humanity
Aspires to the bliss infinite;
The harmony of all the voices and thoughts
Sustains the song of peace,
That heals the broken souls
And enlivens the human goals
In the greater interest of the creation;
Religion never divides,
Neither does it let anyone die;
Rather, it facilitates the realization
Of the divine essence
Of every being;
And it causes the sense of life
To explore the truth beyond all strife!

●●

"Religion facilitates the realization of the divine essence of every being"

Possibility

It's never too late
To dream, to try,
And to be your best version;
It's never too late,
You still can do it,
If you think you can,
You are the master of your thoughts
And your thoughts make your destiny;
You just need to get hold of yourself,
And believe in your tremendous powers
Nothing is impossible,
With a colossal commitment
Leading to persistent efforts;
Nothing can ever impede your progress
Once you start loving the journey
And start to learn
From every single experience;
Things may come and things may go,
But live your goals
In every moment
To make your days in a row!

●●

"You are the master of your thoughts, and your thoughts make your destiny"

Emotions

When someone forgets you,
Don't feel bad,
Don't feel hurt,
Don't curse your heart either;
Rather, keep your purity and positivity intact
Remember all the good memories,
In the shine of the smiles,
Scattered across the ebbs of the emotions;

When someone forgets you
Don't react
Since everyone is unique
In their own ways;
When you start expecting
You are making a serious mistake,
Rise above such weaker thoughts
And wake up to yourself;
Nothing can dismay you from within
You are what you think
Never feel low or downcast;
When you lose something
Inseparably dear,
Know your own value
And keep moving forward;

Relationship is no fun
It's not everyone's cup of tea
If someone plays
You better sit back and enjoy,
Never bother yourself;
Moments grow into experience
And experiences let us grow,
Let them forget
But, never forget the moments
That once occasioned your happiness;
Rather, stay ever thankful
For now you are wise and enlightened!

••

"Moments grow into experiences; and experiences let us grow"

Relationship

Relationship is not just a word;
Rather, it's a feeling
That consists in
Love, understanding,
Trust and sacrifice;
Relationship is the blood
Of every life,
That can alleviate all strife
And enhance the beauty
Of the journey
Involving the purity of the duties;
Relationship smiles
With the sensitive hearts
That beat for each other's souls;
Relationship, in its essence,
Leads to a subtler experience
Of the life's valued goals!

●●

"Relationship consists in love, understanding, trust and sacrifice"

Smile

Let's start the journey
With a smile on the face,
Love in the heart,
And gratitude in the attitude;

Let's try to
Erase all the bad memories
From the mind
And forgive those behind them;
Life is precious
The happiness is what matters ultimately,
Let's learn to be happy
Beyond the dawn of the desire,
Let's explore our best versions
To trounce all despair;
Let's enjoy the moments
Without any attachment
Life is all about moving forward
With the taste of the tests
And celebrating the journey with smiles
Today and forever!

●●

"Life is all about celebrating the journey with smiles today and forever"

My Body

I am what my body is
It makes me feel myself,
It carries my dreams
And creates the power to chase them,
From within and without;
My body sustains all my emotions
And all my conscious and unconscious behavior;
My foremost duty
Is to make my body happy;

Just like I always want to be,
Health is the real happiness,
My body needs my care,
But I keep scarcely aware;
I need to remember
My body is my best friend
It never leaves me till the very end;

People may come
And people may go,
But my body remains a constant companion,
Bearing with me in every situation;
I must take care of my body
The way I care for my loved ones,

Since the safer and healthier it is,
The happier I will be!

● ●

"My body remains a constant companion, bearing with me in every situation"

Black Eagle Books

www.blackeaglebooks.org
info@blackeaglebooks.org

Black Eagle Books, an independent publisher, was founded as a nonprofit organization in April, 2019. It is our mission to connect and engage the Indian diaspora and the world at large with the best of works of world literature published on a collaborative platform, with special emphasis on foregrounding Contemporary Classics and New Writing.

www.ingramcontent.com/pod-product-compliance
Lightning Source LLC
Chambersburg PA
CBHW060620080526
44585CB00013B/917